THE EPIC STORY OF
DAV PILKEY

How a comic writer made kids love reading

GAVIN RILEY

All rights reserved. No part of this publication may be reproduced, distributed, or transmitted in any form or by any means, including photocopying, recording, or other electronic or mechanical methods, without the prior written permission of the publisher, except in the case of brief quotations embodied in critical reviews and certain other noncommercial uses permitted by copyright law.

Copyright © Gavin Riley, 2025.

TABLE OF CONTENT

INTRODUCTION	**3**
CHAPTER ONE	**9**
A Kid with a Wild Imagination	9
CHAPTER TWO	**16**
Finding Comfort in Comics	16
CHAPTER THREE	**23**
A Life-Changing Challenge	23
CHAPTER FOUR	**29**
College Days and a Big Break	29
CHAPTER FIVE	**35**
The Journey to Becoming an Author	35
CHAPTER SIX	**41**
Captain Underpants Takes the World by Storm	41
CHAPTER SEVEN	**48**
From Hard Times to Happy Endings	48
CHAPTER EIGHT	**53**
Dog Man and the Power of Friendship	53
CHAPTER NINE	**59**
Inspiring Kids Everywhere	59
CHAPTER TEN	**65**
Create Like Dav!	65
CONCLUSION	**70**

INTRODUCTION

"You have to first learn to embrace and enjoy your folly if you are to be creative." -Dav Pilkey

The class was embroiled in a conflict. While some kids found mathematical problems to be the enemy, others saw the pressure of tests to be the foe. For Dav Pilkey, though, the hardest aspect was not the actual classes but rather the need to sit still for a long enough period to hear them. His legs were jumping under the table. Writing, his fingers tapped on the notebook. Words from the teacher came and went in his mind, acting as background noise to the stories unfolding there. It happened again after that. David! Out in the corridor, he shouted. When the door slammed shut behind him, Dav found himself alone by himself.

Once again. The corridor was not just known to him; it had also turned into his second class. It was a site where imagination replaced instructional resources and where time appeared to go on forever. Sitting on the cold floor, he pulled out his pencil and let his ideas take charge. He brought his characters to life in the margins of his notebook pages. It's a superhero in briefs.

The toilets that speak. Jokers who play practical jokes on others. Furthermore, the most crucial element would be a world in which children like him, children who did not fit the standard, could be the main characters in their tales. Dav was oblivious at the time that the "punishments" he had endured would develop into his most precious gift. He wasn't just writing; he was creating designs. He wasn't wasting time; he was developing a skill that would eventually make him one of the most loved authors of children's books in the whole world. His struggles with dyslexia and attention-deficit/hyperactivity disorder (ADHD) did not mute him; instead, they gave him the loudest and most colorful voice imaginable. That voice would eventually shape how millions of children saw reading, creativity, and even themselves.

The path of Dav Pilkey is richer than just that of a writer. Every child who has ever felt as though they did not fit in a school shares this tale. Every child who found reading books boring, who struggled to sit still, and who felt school was a place of limits rather than possibilities. The narrative of parents who worried about their child's future and questioned whether they would ever find a way to succeed is this one. It is the story of teachers who saw potential in students deemed unqualified. This is a story showing that often the very traits that distinguish us from others are also the ones that distinguish us as exceptional. For many years, kids were expected to read books. They were assigned, examined, and finally dissected until all of the enjoyment had been drained. Then, though, Dav Pilkey showed up. His books urged kids to laugh rather than to take themselves seriously. Young children were not told to stay sitting; instead, they were urged to jump up and down in joy.

Dav turned reading from a chore to a clandestine club where frivolity was not only allowed but embraced using his absurd humor, strange plots, and comic-book style. He accomplished this by making reading seem like a private club. Still, he worked for his success. On any level, reading was not a joyful experience for me as a kid. The letters seemed to be moving across the page. He was not particularly good at keeping his focus. Teachers did not view him as a storyteller but more as a diversion. The future made his parents anxious. Like many other kids with learning challenges, he was brought up to think his struggles were a flaw, something to be fixed.

He built a cosmos that was distinctively his, though, instead of trying to fit into a reality not meant for him. Decades later, when kids grab a book from the

Captain Underpants or Dog Man series, they don't just see a narrative; they see themselves in the characters. The data they see shows that being different is not a flaw but rather a strength. that they are not defined by their failures, setbacks, or challenges; instead, it is what they do with those hurdles that define them. The issue of how to pique children's interest in reading has been hotly debated among teachers, parents, and literacy experts for ages.

More organized classes? Less strict reading assignments, correct? Any other tests? Dav Pilkey found the solution, nevertheless, in an unexpected place: fun. His books not only teach kids to read but also motivate them to do so. More than anything else, this is what has helped him to have a remarkable impact. Results from a 2019 poll on children's reading habits revealed that over two-thirds of them would read more if they found novels they liked. Students who found reading challenging had an even higher number. The same study finds that one of the main factors kids pick books on their own is their enjoyment of reading. Dav Pilkey built his whole career on this fact; it was not enough for him to just exploit it. His writings have been recognized for changing kids who had hitherto shunned reading into enthusiastic readers. They have given kids who had hitherto shunned reading a reason to stay up late, laughing under the covers with a flashlight. Not only those who struggle with reading but also others who find his work fascinating.

Teachers have found that even the most sophisticated students consume his books, which proves that comedy and narrative can captivate all various types of children. Once regarded as "not real books," his graphic novels' format has developed into one of the most potent weapons in the domain of modern literacy education. Once deemed too trivial, the novel Captain Underpants was banned from schools; now it is being utilized as a gateway to reading. But maybe the most convincing proof of Dav's influence on their life comes from the children themselves. Young followers have sent him letters, emails, and even fan art detailing how his books have affected their lives.

Tell how they went from hating the time set aside for reading to begging for extra time. How he inspired them to find their love of sketching and narrative. For the first time, they saw a culture in which being different was not only acceptable but something to take pride in. Dav Pilkey is more than just a writer; he is a voice for children struggling. His presence shows they are not by themselves. that the challenges people encounter need not define who they are. It can be that the very traits that distinguish them from others are also the ones that make them outstanding.

CHAPTER ONE

A Kid with a Wild Imagination

Though for young Dav Pilkey, Cleveland, Ohio, a small town, was a playground brimming with possibilities, it may not seem like the place where a future literary genius was born. Born on March 4, 1966, Dav was a kid with an incredibly vivid mind that seemed to never stop functioning. Dav filled every available square inch of paper with crazy and bizarre ideas, sketching superheroes, dreaming up hilarious scenarios, and always creating. Dav was always inventing while other kids were happy to play outside or watch TV. Though he was young, it was clear Dav was not like other kids. He had all the qualities of a creative spark that couldn't be contained, boundless energy, and an unquenchable sense of humor.

His family observed this early on, especially when he couldn't spend five minutes without creating a new character or cracking a joke that caused all to chuckle. Even as a little child, he seemed to have a unique viewpoint on the world. He appeared to view the world through a different lens, one in which anything was possible and laws, especially the dull ones, were meant to be twisted just even slightly. Dav's enthusiasm for storytelling was not the outcome of any set school assignments or activities. Like breathing, it was something he felt on a basic level, something that came to him naturally. He was not happy to just read tales; instead, he wanted to create them himself. His notebooks were crammed with silly tales about superheroes and mischievous kids outsmarting adults, comic strips, and doodling. His journals were also packed with comic strips. His ideas were not just scribbles; they were unfiltered windows into his imagination.

David and Barbara Pilkey, his parents, were nice and supportive of their son's unique viewpoint on the world. They never tried to convince him to fit a certain mold. By contrast, they let him investigate his imagination in any way they felt fit. If that was his wish, they let him draw for hours nonstop. They urged him to use toys to act out narratives when he showed desire. They knew their son was especially different, but instead of seeing it as a difficulty, they decided to accept it. Dav's home life provided him with a strong support system that ultimately determined all. His parents never let him feel ashamed, no matter how hard he battled in school or how much he was the child who couldn't sit still. Rather than trying to suppress his creativity, they built a space where he could be himself, and more importantly, they supported his artistic projects.

Though the rest of the world had not yet figured out what he could do, they knew he had something special. Conversely, the world following his departure from his home was not as welcoming. In school, where Dav's zeal, sense of humor, and creative talents sometimes got him into trouble, the circumstances were different.

Dyslexia and attention-deficit/hyperactivity disorder (ADHD) were two conditions that made conventional education very difficult for Dav. The concept of staying still in a classroom appeared impossible. His thoughts would race faster than the lesson being taught, making it impossible for him to focus on the words on the page; it was like trying to hold onto a slippery fish. No matter how much effort he put into it, he just could not absorb information in the same way as other kids. Reading was challenging, writing was challenging, and listening to long lectures seemed like agony. Both of these tasks were difficult. Though their best attempts, his instructors did not always grasp him. At a time when learning disabilities were not as widely investigated or addressed as they are now, children like Dav were often labeled "troublemakers." He had all these traits: his inability to sit still, his propensity to make funny comments at inopportune moments, and his inclination to doodle in his notebook rather than take notes. Most of the time, he was punished for being disruptive instead of being acknowledged for his inventiveness.

Being sent out into the corridor of the building became a frequent component of his educational day. Dav was regarded as a distraction; he would sit alone outside the classroom while other kids labored at their desks. But instead of letting these emotions of loneliness destroy him, he decided to see it as a chance. Should he be unable to attend the class, he would create his universe brimming with great heroes, funny villains, and tales that made him laugh out loud. Captain Underpants was born on this site. Sitting outside the class, Dav used his imagination to transmute his annoyance into something fun.

His idea was of a superhero who ran in his underwear, rescuing the day most absurdly rather than wearing a luxurious cloak or high-tech gadgets. He created George and Harold, two naughty kids. These kids reminded him of himself; they were kids who didn't fit in, kids who liked playing pranks rather than completing assignments, and kids who saw the whole planet as a joke. These people helped him to escape and to turn his challenges into something useful. Though school remained difficult, Dav found ways to survive. Though he was feeling stressed, he used his sense of humor to help his peers laugh. Every boring task became something he could enjoy by sketching jokes and pictures in the margins of his documents. Using painting as a medium of self-expression, he showed that even if he couldn't learn in the same manner as others, he could still succeed in his special way. Despite the challenges he encountered, Dav never lost his love for storytelling.

He might have struggled to read books, but that didn't mean he didn't like reading them. His choice was for comics, which were stories in which words and pictures cooperated to produce a narrative more accessible and engaging to read. He discovered that this medium spoke to him in a way that conventional texts could never. It was his starting point in the narrative universe. The only thing that changed was the way he handled the difficulties he had in school; they never truly vanished. He embraced the way his brain worked rather than let his dyslexia and attention deficit hyperactivity disorder (ADHD) define him. He was not naturally still, followed rigorous orders, or learned in the same way as others. But he had a natural gift for artistic expression, humor, and storytelling. Though some teachers saw him as a distraction, others saw his promise. A few exceptional teachers backed his work; they saw value in his creativity and helped him accept he was not just a "bad student" but a kid with great ability. Their support, together with his parents' unrelenting confidence in him, gave him the confidence to keep drawing and take artistic chances. Several years later, when Dav became a writer, he set out to pen stories for kids like him. These were kids who felt that they weren't smart enough, kids who needed humor to stay interested, and kids who struggled with reading. His compositions ignored the norms usually linked with children's literature. They all had absurd humor, action, and comics. Most essential, they were designed to make kids laugh, so entertaining them and, more critically, motivating them to wish to read. Looking back, it is clear beyond doubt that the difficulties Dav Pilkey faced as a boy were not obstacles but rather the same ones that led to his current status as a novelist. His boundless energy, inability to sit still, and vibrant creativity were not considered shortcomings. He carried his strongest strengths. His efforts have helped millions of children to see and value their uniqueness, to see the power in their creative potential, and to know that, no matter how much they suffer, they can achieve something extraordinary.

CHAPTER TWO

Finding Comfort in Comics

Dav Pilkey likely had no idea that picking up a pencil for the first time to sketch would change the path of his life forever. At first, it was merely something he liked; it was a straightforward approach to killing time when his mind was racing too fast for the world around him. But with time, drawing changed into more than just that. It became his refuge, his escape, the one place he could be himself free from concern about the rules, the expectations, or the frustration he had at school. For a child with attention-deficit/hyperactivity disorder (ADHD) and dyslexia, the classroom was a continual source of trouble. All of these activities seemed like a tremendous amount of effort: standing still, reading long passages, and keeping up with classes that appeared to move at an unreasonably fast speed. But, sketching? Drawing seemed only logical. There were no rules and no incorrect responses. All this is a blank page with limitless choices.

Dav never really felt alone, even when he was punished for rowdy behavior and sent out into the hallway. During quiet periods, he could entertain himself by filling his mind with tales and people that amused him. With only a few pencil strokes, he could design a whole adventure under his control where anything might happen and the only limits were the boundaries of the paper (the actual paper). Funny superhero was among the first characters he ever created; it would also be the one that eventually became Captain Underpants. Dav was already sketching out the exploits of this ridiculous hero wearing only his undies in second grade. Long before he ever thought of starting the writing industry, this was. His early drawings were not perfect or polished, but they were nonetheless lovely. It was a nice time.

Those items amused him. Most crucial is that they gave him a means to convey all the ideas and thoughts running through his head at the moment. In a brief while, his notebooks overflowed with doodling. Among the people were foolish youngsters who found themselves in several situations, talking animals, and insane villains. He wrote tales in which the underdog always triumphed, adventures loaded with pranks, and epic battles between good and evil. For him, comics were more than just a source of entertainment; they were also a way he processed his emotions. If he was feeling frustrated, he could create a character that would have a stupid enemy symbolizing his problems. Should he believe the school was unjust, he might think about two annoying kids outsmarting their strict supervisor. His drawings let him see reality again in a way that was more fun, hilarious, and adventurous than it was. Drawing was a link to something more important, not just a way to escape. Though he struggled with conventional literature, comic books, and cartoons offered him a whole new universe of possibilities. Unlike long paragraphs of thick prose, comics split stories into smaller, more digestible pieces along with images that guide the reader through the narrative.

The mix of words and images made reading seem possible and even enjoyable. Dav, who grew up, realized that the classic comedy and action-packed thrill of the cartoons and comics drew him in. He read every issue of Mad Magazine he could get his hands on; the caustic humor and strange drawings there made him laugh out loud. Created by Charles Schulz, his favorite cartoon was Peanuts, which had a slapstick comedy flair. In this cartoon, adults were only whispers in the background; children were the rulers of the planet. Then came the superhero comics, which told stories of superheroes, larger-than-life battles, and the most theatrical administration of justice. Great Charles Schulz, whose paintings of Charlie Brown and Snoopy were both simple and expressive, was one of Dav's most important sources of motivation. These drawings showed Dav a vital truth: comics did not have to be very complicated or serious to be effective. Sometimes all it took to produce something memorable was a few well-placed lines, a strong personality, and a good sense of humor. Another major impact was Bill Watterson's Calvin and Hobbes children's book series.

Dav related to the story of a child always getting into trouble and his toy tiger who ended out to be his closest friend. Calvin's wild imagination, his refusal to fit in, and his ability to turn even the most boring events into an epic adventure all struck me as somewhat similar. The kind of storytelling that Dav had always imagined himself being able to produce—something that seemed real yet was larger than life. Apart from comic books, animated series and vintage animations also intrigued Dav. From the over-the-top antics of Looney Tunes characters like Bugs Bunny and Daffy Duck, he discovered the power of visual comedy.

He discovered how well-timed quips, fast-paced action, and exaggerated expressions could bring a narrative to life. His understanding of comedy was shaped by Rocky and Bullwinkle's wit and wittiness, The Muppets' ingenuity, and even The Three Stoogers' cheerful nonsense. Still, it wasn't just the comedy that stayed in his thoughts. These cartoons and comics sent a clear message: enjoyment was vital. A narrative did not always have to be serious or educational for it to have any relevance. Sometimes all it took was to make them laugh. When Dav's parents saw he liked drawing, they did something that would be a game-changer: they encouraged him to follow his interests. When many people would have told a kid to stop doodling and focus on "real work," they let him freely explore his creative potential without any limits.

They did not compel him to stay still for long periods, to act like other youngsters, or to stop making jokes. Conversely, they ensured he had lots of pencils and paper and allowed him to create. Certainly, that assistance was really necessary. His parents saw the worth of his work and did not see it as just a distraction, so he could keep his resolve to follow his creative pursuits. His parents never wavered in their faith in him even in times when he felt inadequate at school, when teachers punished him for being different, and even when the world seemed to be telling him that his way of thinking was wrong. He also included his teachers in this motivation. Some found his constant drawing to be an issue; others praised it as a skill. A few special education teachers could get past the hyperactivity and distractions to understand that Dav wasn't just scribbling for fun; rather, he was telling stories. Instead of trying to suppress his creative talent, these teachers found ways to encourage it. One particular teacher had a major impact on him. She didn't scold him for sketching in class; instead, she urged him to write his book so he could release it. He still thought about those little things, those little recognitions of his skills.

A seed was planted in his head during this event: maybe, just maybe, he could turn his enthusiasm for comics into something real. Though Dav's painting skills got better with age, he always maintained his sense of humor and sense of play. Though his style changed and became more polished, his work always had exaggerated emotions, fast-paced action, and humorous storylines. Growing his love of comics led him to daydream about the chance to write his books, tales children of his age would genuinely want to read. Everything he produces shows the impact of those early inspirations. All of these components, from the clever humor of Mad Magazine to the wicked energy of Calvin and Hobbes to the simple yet expressive style of Peanuts, found their way into his work. The most crucial thing he learned from his boyhood idols, however, was that stories should be fun to tell. Where was the point if it did not make youngsters laugh and if it did not give them any kind of amusement? Such an attitude would drive his whole professional existence. Though he may have created novels that seemed like homework, he instead wrote ones that seemed like a party. Rather than penning tales heavy with long descriptions, he created visually appealing, fast, funny encounters. Moreover, instead of following the traditional rules for writing for children, he violated them in the most efficient way possible. When one reflects on the past, it is easy to see how drawing saved Dav Pilkey. For him, the activity was more than just a hobby; it was his way of understanding the world, of turning his frustration into laughter, and of finding happiness in the moments when all else appeared to be too much. Most importantly, it was the thing that would eventually guide him to his greatest goal: to write books that motivated millions of children to fall in love with reading, just as comics had done for him in the past.

CHAPTER THREE

A Life-Changing Challenge

For young Dav Pilkey, getting into trouble was not exactly a rare event. That almost happened daily. The tight framework of the classroom seemed like an impossible cage at the same time that his mind was racing from one idea to the next. Not being able to move was agony. Sitting through long lectures was exhausting. Finding the will to resist the desire to jest at the most inappropriate moment, too? That was quite improbable.

The teachers did all they could to keep Dav in line, but he was not the sort of child who could readily fit inside the system. He had no desire to be challenging; he just couldn't stop thinking. His energy at school was so great that it occasionally didn't match what was expected of him. Whenever a lesson ran on for an unreasonably long time, his hands would begin to move on their own and he would sketch tiny doodles in the margins of his notebook. Should a teacher ask for class quiet, he usually said something funny just before he could stop himself. Should he be told to focus on reading, his mind would quickly drift to the tales he wanted to create instead. Eventually, his teachers ran out of patience. Though she probably didn't know it at the time, his teacher decided at some point in time that his disruptions were intolerable and would change the direction of his life. She let him out into the open down the corridor. Many kids would see this as a kind of punishment, a moment of embarrassment. On the other hand, for Dav, it proved to be a very different encounter. The location became his artistic area. The policies he had to obey had no strings attached; there were no workbooks to complete and no teachers chastising him for doodling in the corridor instead of concentrating. All that was there was him, his thoughts, and a blank page of paper. That was all he needed to do. During his free time, first, he did nothing but sketch. Drawing funny characters, dreaming crazy action scenarios, and letting his creativity run riot all helped him to free his imagination. But the more he sketched, the more he realized he wasn't only creating arbitrary ink and water designs. He told a story. Dav chose to see the situation as a chance rather than let it shame him that he was expelled from class. Should he be unable to attend the class, he would create his replacement. Should he be denied access to the learning environment, he might build his universe. Every time he found himself in the corridor, which was very often, he added to his stories by inventing new characters and thinking of things that made him laugh. At some point in time, a new sort of superhero also emerged in that specific corridor. Though he loved superheroes, Dav also liked mocking them. He saw, given the constant inclusion of dramatic backstories, high-tech gadgets, and dark, brooding personalities, that most superhero narratives took themselves rather seriously. But what if there was a superhero exactly opposite to what we usually observe? Think about the chance that he was utterly foolish, silly, and ludicrous. At that precise time, he realized Captain Underpants. Someone who was a superhero who wore tighty-whises instead of a cape. A hero without any high-tech weapons but with an outrageous amount of enthusiasm. someone who battled crime who wasn't exactly the strong or the most clever but who somehow saved the day in every single case. It was the perfect idea, the sort of silly, off-the-wall character that made him laugh so much he felt compelled to keep drawing.

Thinking about the most absurd things that could happen there, Dav began sketching out the adventures Captain Underpants would go on. He showed two kids who usually cause trouble: George and Harold. They were often making their comedy and playing pranks on one another. His inventiveness produced the bizarre foes, the ridiculous plots, and the action scenes more akin to slapstick comedy than to conventional superhero fights. Initially, sketching Captain Underpants was just a pleasurable pastime. Dav, however, discovered as he kept at it that it became more and more important to him. This was not just another doodle he had scrawled in the margins of his notebook; rather, it was a character with personality, humor, and the sort of energy akin to his own. His colleagues soon took notice. Sitting next to him, children would look over his shoulder to see him filling his notepad with the latest adventure of Captain Underpants. Passing his comics around the class like hidden treasures, they pleaded with him to let them read them.

Turning the pages of the book, the kids would chuckle at the ridiculousness of the scenario, and their laughter would ripple over the whole room. Incredible as it may seem, Dav came to understand he was not the only one who liked this specific type of comedy. The book completely enthralled all of his classmates, including those who usually had a strong interest in reading. They wanted more of it. A little bit more was needed. And it was then that Dav first started to grasp how much his stories could affect others. Though his colleagues loved his comics, not everyone shared that view. Some instructors were not entertained. They thought Captain Underpants to be just another excuse for

Dav's lack of focus in class and a further diversion. To them, it was not narrative but rather a lot of goofing off. But his parents viewed the situation differently. Though parents knew their son struggled academically, they also knew how much art made him happy. Not once did they advise him to cease creating. Rather, they discovered means to support him. He was free to be himself; his creativity could flow wild without any effort to fit him into an unsuitable mold. In everything, that assistance was the deciding element. It kept him working hard even when school looked like an insurmountable challenge.

He found the confidence to keep creating stories that not only amused him but also others around him via sketching and writing. Years later, when he finally got around to converting Captain Underpants into a published book, he added something important at the front: a dedication to all the kids who have ever felt different, distracted, or misunderstood. primarily because he was so familiar with the experience of being that child—the one who couldn't stay still, who struggled in school, and who got in trouble just for being themselves. Captain Underpants has more to offer than simply being a funny superhero. A child with a wild imagination, a notebook, and a pencil waiting in the hallway could create something original. He was proof that imagination might come from anywhere.

CHAPTER FOUR

College Days and a Big Break

In his wildest thoughts, Dav Pilkey never imagined himself in college. School had always been a battle for him, and this was a place where he felt out of place instead of motivated. But, despite the challenges he had in the classroom, one thing had been constant all his life: his love of storytelling. He knew that whatever route he chose after high school graduation would need him to be inventive. This choice led him to Kent State University, which is famous for its strong writing and arts programs. It was the first time in his life that he had experienced this surrounded by people who shared his passion for art, narrative, and humor. For him, college was not easy; he battled the same issues that had made his entire life difficult in school.

There was, nevertheless, one major distinction between the two. He was free to follow his passions. Dav's desire to be creative often got him into trouble while he was in high school. Conversely, it was lauded in college. He no longer had to attend courses he found uninteresting; rather, he could choose ones consistent with his creative preferences. He studied art, tried out different writing techniques, and surrounded himself with innovative people who motivated him to expand his concepts. But this did not imply that everything was going well. He had never been used to focusing, deadlines, and discipline, yet in college he was still expected to practice all three. Keeping up with the assignments was challenging, and enduring long lectures still seemed like an insurmountable feat. Conversely, unlike elementary and high school, this environment was different in that individuals were not trying to change him in any manner. His instructors not only failed to punish him for being too excited or sidetracked, but they actively urged him to direct that drive into his creative projects. Dav's notebook drawings were beyond counting. He filled them with drawings that made him chuckle, fresh characters, and ideas for funny stories. He was preparing to be an artist, not just a student. Through the process of trial and error, he was honing his craft and discovering what worked (and what did not).

One of the most crucial things he learned while at Kent State was the understanding that delivering a story was about connecting with an audience, not only about drawing funny pictures. He started to think more about the things that caught kids' interest, the things that made them laugh, and the sorts of novels he would have liked to read as a child. He started to understand when writing books for kids that the very qualities that had once made education difficult for him—his little attention span, his passion for humor, and his reluctance to sit still for long periods—were also strengths. While attending Kent State, Dav helped himself by doing several odd jobs. These jobs ranged from warehouse work to dishwashing. Though those jobs were somewhat demanding, he always came back to his true love: story writing. He had no idea how to get there, but he was determined to make it a profession.

He was set on making it his lifetime labor. All at once, everything changed. At some point, Dav came upon details on a nationwide book competition available to would-be authors of children's books. Sponsored by the publishing company Scholastic, the competition's winner would get a publishing deal. The competition was seeking fresh talent; the winner would get something nearly too wonderful to live. For Dav to take part in, it was more than simply a contest. It was a chance. With nothing to lose, he threw himself into the task and labored relentlessly to create a book that would stand out from the crowd. To be successful, he knew he had to produce something that not only showed his sense of humor but also related to kids. Apart from being inspired by the difficulties he had gone through as a child, he chose to pen a book extolling the virtues of imagination, mischief, and creativity. Ultimately, he created World War Won, a clever and funny narrative highlighting his unique perspective on storytelling. Full of humor, action, and the sort of unexpected vitality that had been a hallmark of his work from the very beginning to now, it was He had no idea what to expect from the publication when he submitted his manuscript. Then came the unthinkable: he triumphed.

The win in the contest was not only a personal success for me. The event that signaled the start of his professional existence. In what appeared to be such a brief period, he moved from being a college student struggling to determine his future to being a published author. The competition was more than just a way for Dav to publish his book. It was proof that his creative talents mattered. He eventually got to this stage after all those years of being in trouble for sketching in class, of feeling like he didn't fit into the conventional educational system, and of questioning whether he would ever discover a place where his ideas were appreciated. The book deal meant his work would be in the hands of real readers post-publication. Children would experience his stories in the same way he had once experienced the comics and cartoons that had inspired him. It was a time that gave him the validation that he was going in the right way. Dav began to understand with the official release of World War Won that this was only the start of something far more important. If he could turn one book into reality, why not do more? Having spent his whole life penning tales, he now had the chance to share them with the rest of the planet. He did not take that chance lightly. He saw his book contract as a source of motivation to continue pushing himself both emotionally and professionally as a writer and artist rather than as a one-time success. Getting published was one thing, but he knew that making a long-lasting impact on readers was something very different.

His early success not only increased his confidence but also taught him a useful lesson: sometimes the qualities that distinguish you from others are the very ones that distinguish you from others. Spending his whole life trying to fit the criteria of a "perfect" student might have blinded him to his real talents. But he had found a means to change the most challenging challenges he confronted into the most potent assets he carried inside by embracing his inventiveness and leaning into the aspects that set him different. Looking back, we see that winning that competition was much more than simply having a book out. It was about showing to himself and to the rest of the world that other people's stories mattered. Certainly, humor was significant. What mattered was inventiveness. Perhaps most importantly, children like him—those who struggled in school, those with active imaginations, and those who sometimes felt as though they didn't quite fit in—deserved to read books that spoke to them. He was going to carry this lesson with him for the rest of his working life, and it would greatly influence everything he would create going forward.

CHAPTER FIVE

The Journey to Becoming an Author

Becoming a successful writer is not a quick process; Dav Pilkey's career was not an exception to this. Winning the national book contest while in college was a great achievement, but it did not ensure quick recognition or a steady job. Indeed, his early years as a writer were full of ups and downs, with times of success followed by somewhat depressing rejections. But Dav never lost sight of the one thing that was most crucial despite all that was happening: producing stories that would make children laugh and enjoy reading. Dav was keen to keep the momentum set after World War Won's release.

Apart from having an endless supply of concepts for fresh books, he was keen to show he was more than just a one-hit marvel. Conversely, it was not easy to join the publishing world. Though his first book had been chosen as the contest victor, his next projects had to fight for a place in an industry growingly competitive and often ambiguous. Though they did not become very profitable, his first few books were well-received. Among his works, names like Dogzilla and Kat Kong showed his love of satire and comedy. These titles referenced legendary monster films while also reflecting his comedic take on narrative. Apart from being creative and funny, these books were full of the unusual vitality that distinguished Dav's work from others. But even if they drew a crowd, they did not push him into celebrity status. The rejections came after that. Though Dav had several concepts, he kept sending manuscript after manuscript to publishers with the aim of getting another chance to engage with possible readers. Still, not every book found a home. Some publications did not understand his sense of humor.

Many individuals were worried that his art was too strange or foolish. Some others lacked the desire to gamble on a new writer who diverged from the traditional pattern. Any writer finds rejection to be a tough experience, but for someone like Dav, who struggled with self-doubt throughout his education and had spent a great part of his life feeling like an outsider, it was particularly difficult. At times, he fought with himself about whether or not he had the required abilities to thrive in the field. Every single rejection taught him something, though. Many publishers replied with polite "no thank you" emails. Others offered helpful comments. Furthermore, he saw every challenge he faced as a chance to evolve and improve. By using his encounters, he was able to enhance his narrative abilities, his sense of humor, and most notably, his capacity to stay genuine about who he is. Among the most crucial things he learned was that success in publishing was not only about skill; it also required tenacity. Should one of his books fail, he would pen another. Should one of his concepts be rejected, he would create a way to enhance the next one. Dav also started to notice the novels kids wanted to read. He knew that kids didn't always like the books adults thought they should like. Often, books targeted at children were too serious, formal, or didactic in a way that seemed unnatural. Dav, on the other hand, went differently.

He wanted his books to feel like something a kid would want to read instead of something they had to read. Eventually, this frame of mind served as the foundation for his distinctive narrative approach. His writings not only included funny material but also sought to make reading fun. His novels' pages were crammed with wacky people, fast-paced narratives, and jokes that made kids laugh so hard they forgot they were reading. It was then that the breakthrough he had been expecting finally appeared. Since childhood, Dav had been writing on a story that had been troubling him. When he was in second grade, the idea for the book had come to him in the corridor of his classroom. It was a tale about a superhero dressed in his undies saving the day most strangely, a principal under hypnosis, and two kids who liked pulling pranks. The one was Mr. Captain Underpants. At first, when he shared the idea with others, not everyone was sold. Is he a superhero only in his underwear? Would you like to read a book encouraging kids to create their comics? Some publishers thought it too ridiculous, too juvenile, and too unlike what was "expected" in children's literature. They believed it surpassed their hopes. Dav, though, had confidence in it. He knew the program Captain Underpants was about celebrating creative expression, not merely about telling stupid jokes. This project aimed to give kids the chance to enjoy books, laugh, and use their imaginations in a way that seemed natural.

The most crucial element is that it was a book he would have liked to read as a kid. Children quickly became familiar with the Captain Underpants series following the first book's long-awaited release. It was everything young readers wanted but didn't always discover in conventional books: the humor, the comics-within-a-book approach, and the interactive experience. Then an amazing incident occurred. For kids who didn't typically like reading, Captain Underpants was a book they sought. The book's popularity sparked a quick, strong desire for further adventures. Dav's years of laborious quest for celebrity were now past; he had at last discovered his audience. What distinguished Captain Underpants from his earlier works was not only the humor but also the relationship it built with its audience. Apart from reading Captain Underpants, kids felt they were part of the narrative. They saw themselves in George and Harold, the naughty yet inventive kids who created their comics. They glanced through the pages, laughed at the exaggerated villains, and scanned the action sequences resembling a flip-o-rama, all of which helped them to fall in love with reading unknowingly. Conversely, Captain Underpants' success changed more than only Dav's work life. This changed his self-image. Over many years, he had been the youngster who struggled in school, the one who got into trouble, and the one who felt he did not belong. Still, at this moment he was the writer who had turned all those events into something positive. The same qualities that had made school difficult for him were his frenzied energy, his passion for comedy, and his constant doodling. But these also turned out to be the qualities that had helped his works succeed. It wasn't only about writing commercially successful novels. Our work was centered on creating significant literature. Throughout his childhood, Dav felt that books were not for kids like him. At this point, he began penning stories for kids who felt similarly. His books resonated with kids with attention-deficit/hyperactivity disorder (ADHD), those who struggled with reading, and those with active imaginations who sometimes found themselves in trouble. Furthermore, by doing so, he was helping them to find joy in something that had previously seemed unreachable. A long road strewn with obstacles and much disappointment had led to publication success. Dav had saved one thing despite all that had occurred: his love of storytelling. He had come to understand that creativity was not something to be controlled but rather something that wanted to be welcomed. And maybe most crucially, he had shown that for books to matter they need not be grave. When he turned reading into a fun activity, Dav Pilkey found his calling. From then on, he was only starting his path as well.

CHAPTER SIX

Captain Underpants Takes the World by Storm

Dav Pilkey was never meant to be a well-known event. When The Adventures of Captain Underpants was initially released and made available to the public, he had no idea it would go on to become one of the most well-liked children's series of all time. But, the instant kids could grasp the first book, an incredible event took place: it shot off like a rocket launch. The funny exploits of George and Harold, the naughty best friends who used their creativity (and a bit of hypnotism) to turn their grumpy principal into the best underwear-clad superhero the world had ever seen, left young readers wanting more. Using their imagination, George and Harold would turn their principal into a superhero.

The book, which was packed with the sort of comedy that made kids laugh uncontrollably, had pranks, wordplay, over-the-top villains, and, of course, a great deal of underwear. Children were not just amused by laughter. Unlike anything else for sale, the book Captain Underpants was an interactive reading experience, not just a traditional chapter book. The story has comic strips laid out to look like something kids would draw. Sections titled "flip-o-rama" turned reading into a thrilling event. By fast flipping the pages back and forth, these areas let kids mimic battles. The last point to keep in mind is the actual telling of stories. Captain Underpants seemed more like a rollercoaster ride when compared to many other children's books, which usually follow orderly and predictable stories. It was frantic, fast-paced, and full of surprises and turns. It may show how kids think and play, including their funny internal jokes, their wild fantasies, and their love of the absurd. But what set Captain Underpants apart from other movies was its heart.

Beneath all the jokes and absurdity lay something more profound: a message that children like George and Harold mattered. Some children did not get perfect grades. The children in question were pranksters, troublemakers, and those who struggled to follow the rules. But, when they focused on anything, they were not just clever and creative but also unrelenting. That idea resonated with the crowd to a great extent. It was as though kids who had never cared about books before suddenly wanted to read. Hurrying to flip the pages of the book, they were eager to learn what strange next occurrence would occur. Many young readers, especially those who struggled with conventional books, discovered that Captain Underpants was the book that unlocked the door to a passion for reading that would endure for all time. Parents and teachers started to notice an unanticipated event. Suddenly, those kids who had previously been hesitant readers—those who found books either boring or too difficult—were choosing to read for happiness. Staying up late, laughing under the covers with a flashlight, and flipping page after page of the book, those kids who had never completed a book before were doing so. Dav had worked his magic to create something very amazing: books that turned reading into a game. Not everyone, though, saw it that way. Controversy has repercussions following Captain Underpants' fast-growing appeal. Parents, teachers, and school authorities among others condemned the series as unsuitable for young readers since it was too funny, too disruptive, or even inappropriate.

Among the most notable criticisms was the claim that George and Harold were bad role models. They disobeyed people in authority, created several trouble, and pranks were perpetrated on them. Some adults were worried that the books might promote disrespect towards staff members and administrators or that children would imitate their behavior after their own. Then, naturally, the absence of underpants created issues. Several critics believed that a superhero roaming around in his underwear was unsuitable for children's books. They said that the comedy was of a lowbrow and juvenile sort and that it was not the sort of content children should be reading. As a result, Captain Underpants was among the books most often questioned in public libraries and schools. Some school systems even banned it, taking it off the shelf or asking parents' permission to use it. Dav had already experienced this with people in power misinterpreting his artistic abilities. His parents ordered him to draw comics in the corridor as a kid. But now that he was grown, his writings were being attacked for the same reason: they did not fit the traditional mold of what some people thought books should be.

On the contrary, Dav, like he had done when he was in school, refused to enable the criticism to discourage him. The writer reinforced his belief that books should be enjoyable, readily available, and written for both youngsters and adults instead of changing his novels to fit the tastes of the critics. He addressed the problem with humor, kindness, and a deep understanding of the value of his writings. Asked about the prohibitions, he often raised a vital question: if a book may arouse a child's curiosity in reading, this is absolutely a good change, don't you agree? He also recounted his encounters, highlighting the reality that at one time in his life, he had been one of those kids who struggled with reading and attention in school. Had he been limited to reading only "serious" books, he might never have discovered how much he loved storytelling. The truth was that the argument only served to raise Captain Underpants' notoriety. More individuals tried to ban it, more kids said they wanted to read it. The book's appeal grew increasingly defined by its defiance; like George and Harold, who were not afraid to break the rules, Captain Underpants would not be limited to a certain genre. The answer helped to underline the point the book was attempting to make: that imagination should not be limited and that comedy is not a bad thing.

Notwithstanding the challenges, the Captain Underpants series kept growing. New books came out, and everyone contributed to the funny escapades George, Harold, and their underpants-wearing hero were having. The series was translated into a variety of various languages and sold millions of copies, therefore demonstrating its great success. It was clear that kids throughout the world related to Dav's tales. An even more important occurrence followed then. Hollywood took notice. After the series had been on the bestseller list for several years, a major animated film adaptation of Captain Underpants was published. Released in 2017, the film brought George, Harold, and their superhero to the big screen, so exposing their world to an even larger audience than there had been previously. Dav was closely involved in the making of the movie to guarantee it stayed true to the essence of the books. Fans greeted it with excitement when it was eventually made public; like the books, it made kids vocalize their laughter. But, even if Captain Underpants became a worldwide sensation, Dav never lost sight of the basic drive that inspired him to start writing in the first place. He was also trying to make reading a fun and empowering experience for kids, not just one that made them giggle. During interviews, he often recounted stories of kids struggling with reading until they found Captain Underpants. Parents would tell him their kids hated reading books until they picked up one of his stories and then found themselves unable to put it down. Teachers said that kids who had once been hesitant readers were now excited to go to the library and eager to start their next journey.

Dav's concept of success was as stated above. Despite the challenges, criticism, and bans he encountered, he was able to achieve his objectives. He had previously authored stories that kids enjoyed reading. The books made them chuckle. They read books reminding them of the value of creativity. Furthermore, by doing this, one superhero who wore underpants at a time changed the way millions of kids read.

CHAPTER SEVEN

From Hard Times to Happy Endings

From the outside, most of the time success seems to be effortless. A writer, Dav Pilkey turned his boyhood mischief into a profession that delighted millions. For his work, he was recognized by the whole world as the beloved author of Captain Underpants. Kids loved his tales, and the laughter he had been punished for in school was now celebrated throughout the world. His tales were popular with kids and his books were flying off the shelves. Conversely, behind the scenes, life was not always easy. Dav had been working too hard for many years to achieve the criteria of success, which included writing book after book, making deadlines, and traveling for events.

Though they had been his escape in the past, drawing, writing, and other artistic pursuits were starting to seem like pressure to him. Though the weight of expectation was becoming more and more, the joy of storytelling remained. Then there was the weariness that accompanied being renowned all along. Dav had never been anybody who wanted the spotlight at any time in his life. As a child, he used to spend a lot of time lost in his universe penning stories that made him happy.

Now everyone on earth was watching. His writings were examined, debated, and even outright banned. The more popular Captain Underpants, the more closely the academic world studied his work. Realizing he had achieved his goal was strange; certain parts of it felt too much. Though he had worked hard to reach this stage, something still fell short. Consequently, he decided to change the direction of all. Dav decided to sit back and concentrate on something different instead of pushing himself to the point of breaking. He decided, after some thought, that he had to first look after himself if he was to keep creating tales that made kids laugh. At that time, he moved to a quiet seaside resort far from the hustle and stress of the publishing sector, one of the most important changes in his life.

The sea had been a safe sanctuary for him for as long as he could remember. The sound of the waves, the great sky, and the seemingly endless horizon all had a quality that helped him maintain his mental order. The lack of distractions let him breathe deeply here. He could consider. Not because he was obligated to, he could create anything he wanted. Moreover, an amazing occurrence happened during this period of self-reflection. Dav discovered love. In this less busy time of his life, he got to know Sayuri, the woman who would one day marry him. Every time they met directly, they felt an immediate link. He was a kind, gifted guy, and Sayuri got him in a manner that quite a few others did. She not only praised his work but also believed in it. Their friendship changed him in ways he had not expected. Dav had been carrying the weight of his early difficulties—including emotions of loneliness, memories of being misunderstood, and doubts that persisted even after he found success—over many years. Conversely, he found with Sayuri a new kind of joy not based on book sales or reviews. Though now he had someone in his life who gave him joy, it had been a major part of his life spent making others laugh.

Her presence in his life not only brought him joy but also helped him to revive his creative energy. With Sayuri by his side, Dav could once more experience the simple joy of storytelling. He was writing because he had found his passion for the work back, not only to meet deadlines. His artwork become more fanciful and his stories more reflective. Over time, she turned into his most passionate supporter, the one who alerted him to the factors driving his initial creation. With this newly discovered sense of balance, he could advance his profession to greater heights. One he started working on during this time frame was a new project that would once again change the terrain of children's literature. He had always loved sketching comics as a child, and he had seen how Captain Underpants had inspired young readers to create their narratives. What if he took that particular concept even further? Dog Man was born at that point. In contrast to Captain Underpants, which mixed comics with conventional narrative, Dog Man was completely shown in comic book form. The narrative was touching, funny, and quite action-packed. It was about a half-dog, half-human hero who battled criminals in the most absurd way imaginable. Conversely, much like Captain Underpants, it wasn't solely about comedy; it had a sentimental side. It had emotion.

At its core, though, it was about the strength of creativity. Dog Man became an instant success the same moment it was made available to the public. Children now had something new to look forward to if they had formerly liked Captain Underpants. But what is even better? The Dog Man series was exposing reading to a new generation of kids. Dav found himself at the center of a literary movement for the second time; yet, this time the event was different. He wasn't just riding the wave of success; he liked it. Having Sayuri by his side helped him to combine his work and personal life. He found time for the things that mattered to him, like traveling the globe, spending time with the people he loved, and yet writing stories that brought joy to those all around. Looking back, it was painfully clear that every fight had led him to this moment. His childhood challenges, the rejections he went through, and the pressures he felt as a result of his fame had all been stepping stones leading to something more important. At this stage, he was living evidence that happiness and invention need not be at odds with one another. Dav Pilkey has not only built a successful business but also a life full of meaning, joy, and purpose. He had done this by looking for himself, by surrounding himself with love and support, and by always remembering the happiness that lay within the craft of narrative.

CHAPTER EIGHT

Dog Man and the Power of Friendship

Though Dav Pilkey had already had a major influence on children's literature with the release of Captain Underpants, he was not yet done. Years of George and Harold's crazy adventures had him another idea: one that would bring an new generation of readers to the delight of reading. He understood how very helpful this would be. Unlike the last time, his work was a dog with the heart of a loyal companion and the energy of a real hero fighting crime rather than a principal who had changed into a superhero.

Dog Man was created in this manner. The idea of Dog Man was not new; in fact, it had been drifting about in Dav's mind for many years. As a child, he would create his comics as well as spend untold hours drawing and creating stories that would make him chuckle. One of the characters he early doodled was Dog Man, a police officer half-dog, half-human who defended his city with a combination of courage and goofiness. Of these figures, he discovered one to be most memorable. Back then, Dog Man was only one of the many characters Dav had dreamed up. But, when he grew older and became a best-selling author, he started to worry about him again. Imagine he could resurrect Dog Man. Imagine for a second that he used all the knowledge he had acquired from Captain Underpants to create something unique. This question catalyzed what would finally become one of the most popular graphic novel series for youngsters. Unlike Captain Underpants, which had a mix of conventional narration and comic strips, Dog Man was a full-fledged graphic book. Every page was packed with action, comedy, and the sort of narrative that gave kids the feeling they were involved in the adventure. The character's design was simple and almost childlike, resembling something a toddler could sketch in the margins of their notebook. That was no accident. Dav thought Dog Man needed to be friendly. Having read hefty, thick chapter books, he knew that some kids felt overwhelmed. He also knew that other kids, especially those with dyslexia, attention-deficit/hyperactivity disorder (ADHD), or other learning challenges, found it hard to relate to conventional books. Conversely, graphic novels can quickly grab a child's mind. Using both images and language, they could elevate the narrative to a visual, pleasurable, and interesting degree. This worked. Children liked Dog Man as soon as it hit shops. They liked the fast-paced action, the ridiculous humor, and the outrageous adventures of a hero who wasn't perfect but always gave it his all. Above all, they loved how Dog Man made them feel: that reading was something they could enjoy regardless of their level of knowledge. The success of Dog Man was not only due to the humor or action; rather, it was the way the book gave kids a feeling of agency. It lacked any patronizing tone. I got the idea it was not something they meant to read. This was one of the items they wanted to read. Those who were hesitant to read found this to be very crucial. Many kids may find reading to be a chore. They may have struggled with it in class. They may have been informed they are "not good at reading." Perhaps they have never seen a book that has captured their attention. Conversely, when they find Dog Man, something changes.

The art grabs their attention fast and keeps it. Short sentences and speech bubbles help to simplify the material greatly. The characters are funny, the jokes are so funny that make them laugh out loud, and the story moves at such a fast speed that they don't even know how much they are reading. After all, that is the magic of Dog Man. It makes kids adore books. Apart from making reading more fun, Dog Man also sends out another important message: the power of friendship. The tale of Dog Man is not just about a hero mostly against criminals. The most essential things are loyalty, compassion, and being there for the individuals—or pets—most important to you. The story emphasizes not just Dog Man's battle against evildoers but also his growth as a friend, a comrade, and a nice guy (or dog). Every book in the series reflects this concept. Whether it's Dog Man's friendship with Li'l Petey, the little kitten with a big heart, or his complicated relationship with Petey, the villain-turned-ally, the stories educate kids that friendship isn't always easy but it's always worth it. Dav is personal about this. Having struggled at school, often feeling misunderstood, and spending much of his life retreating into his fantasy, he knows the value that friendship can have. His books, therefore, are not simply about making kids laugh; they are also about making them feel as though they are being seen. Consequently, he knows that some of his readers could be struggling as well. Maybe they feel alienated in class. Maybe they have been informed they are not entitled to extra. Maybe all they need is a simple nudge to remember their significance. Dav gives kids via Dog Man a hero who isn't perfect but keeps trying, who makes mistakes but learns from them, and who reminds them that creativity and generosity are also gifts. But Dog Man's impact goes far deeper. Graphic novels' rising appeal is prompting more and more parents and educators to see them not only as a source of pleasure but also as powerful literacy tools. In the past, some people claimed that graphic novels did not constitute "real books." They were afraid that the fact that they included pictures made them significantly less helpful than traditional novels. Research, on the other hand, has shown the opposite: graphic novels help children acquire good reading skills. Why? They excite the brain in many different ways. Children reading a graphic novel are not just decoding the language but also grasping the images, tracking the visual narrative's hints, and linking the text to the images. Doing so helps them to develop their vocabulary, strengthen their understanding of what they read, and sharpen their critical thinking skills. For children who struggle with reading, graphic novels could be life-changing. They reduce the reader's fearsome impact of big text blocks. Their knowledge of the visual backdrop helps them to understand the story more clearly. Often, a lack of confidence is the main barrier keeping kids from becoming good readers. Dav's work has been all the more important for this reason. He is not just writing books; he is also enabling children who would have otherwise ignored the practice to read more easily. His achievements have also opened the way for new graphic novels appropriate for kids. This goes beyond Dog Man. Publishers are hoping to fund more stories akin to his as a result of his work. More and more writers and artists are creating books that are fun, fascinating, and thrilling to read. More and more kids are picking up books not because they have to but because they want to. Ultimately, that is precisely what Dav's work has always been about: not only creating stories but also inspiring kids to grow a passion for reading. Dog Man is another of his successes. He has created a hero who is both nice and brave. It is a book that is both important and fun. Furthermore, an amazing as well as reasonable reading experience.

CHAPTER NINE

Inspiring Kids Everywhere

From the start of his career, Dav Pilkey has maintained that books should not only teach kids how to read but also motivate them to desire to read. His books have exactly done this for many kids throughout the world. From Captain Underpants to Dog Man, the tales he has penned have turned many who were uninterested in reading into passionate readers. Children who once loathed reading are now racing through his graphic novels, laughing out loud at every page and eagerly looking forward to the arrival of the following edition. Many individuals complete his works on their own, reading them for the first time. For some people, they are the cause of their initial reading. It should so be expected that parents and teachers often call him a "literary superhero." But how much has he been able to inspire so many young readers? The explanation lies in his approach to reading, which emphasizes enjoyment over effort. How to Turn Reading into an Enjoyable Activity Dav knows that kids don't like to read anything that gives them the impression they are working. Many readers struggle connect books with annoyance by complaining about long paragraphs, challenging vocabulary, and uninteresting stories. Conversely, everything changes when they grab a Dav Pilkey book. From the very first page, his books are packed with humor and adventure; they run at a dizzying pace and are thrilling. Though still full of life, the text is basic and clear, which helps young readers to grasp it. By splitting the lines with vibrant images that make each page feel like a happy experience, he narrates stories in a comic book style, hence keeping kids engaged. When children are exposed to a mix of short, punchy sentences and expressive artwork, they are more likely to feel successful when reading. Children who feel successful are driven to keep working. Students start to believe in their reading skills. Many professors use his works in their classes as a result. The teachers have seen personally how kids who had previously battled with reading get more excited about reading when they read novels like Dog Man or Captain Underpants. The books help children to understand that they can like reading and to acquire confidence. Parents of children have also seen this change. Many parents have similar stories about how their kids, especially those with attention-deficit/hyperactivity disorder (ADHD), dyslexia, or other learning challenges, went from shunning books to pleading for more reading time. Some people say Dav's books were the first ones their kids ever read from start to finish. The strength of his works is not only from the language and illustrations of his stories. They influence how kids feel. Humor's Strength Dav Pilkey's narratives have always been focused on the usage of comedy as a key component. He believes that not only is comedy good for kids, but it is quite essential for them. Laughter helps kids to unwind and lower their defenses. Reading seems more like a kind of enjoyment than a task connected to education. Furthermore, should children start to link books with joy, they will be far more likely to keep reading by themselves. This explains why both Captain Underpants and Dog Man are overflowing with ludicrous humor, wacky people, and outlandish scenarios. From a dog with a large heart battling crime to a principal who becomes a superhero while wearing undies, Dav's characters may make kids giggle and sense of understanding. He can remember what it was like to be a kid who battled focus in class and who was always in trouble for excessive laughter. He went through everything. He knows some kids feel they don't fit in the traditional education system. His tales are more than simply amusing because of this; they resonate with kids who have the feeling of being on the outside looking in. His stories make it very clear that it is okay to be stupid. Laughing is allowed. Being unique is not negative. Dav's books, nevertheless, provide something even more profound: the ability to turn obstacles into assets. The Creative Superpowers One Dav has always been open about his struggles with dyslexia and attention-deficit/hyperactivity disorder (ADHD). The school was hard for him as a kid. His disruptive conduct often got him sent to the corridor. He felt he was unfit for traditional schooling. But instead of letting those difficulties define him, he decided to use them. He could sketch comics during his corridor time. Having ADHD made his imagination more active. Having dyslexia made him see the world differently. But instead of quitting, he turned his challenges into chances for invention, and that is the lesson he wishes kids to also acquire. He inspires kids to embrace their creative side despite the obstacles they are facing using the books he writes. He shows pupils that creativity is a useful tool, not just a pleasurable hobby. A range of creative outlets—including writing, drawing, acting, and any other such activity—allows children to turn their ideas into something amazing. This is why he often urges kids to create their comics. Most of his books have "how-to-draw" sections that guide kids through the process of drawing their favorite characters in a step-by-step fashion. The activities and comic book templates on his website help children to write their own stories. He also plans activities where he teaches kids to build their heroes. His deeds not only inspire students to read but also inspire them to make. He also wants them to know that their ideas matter. the reality that their stories merit telling. They need not be "perfect" in painting or writing to produce something extraordinary. Furthermore, kids have reacted in the most favorable way possible by grabbing pencils and creating their universes. Using Imagination's Strength to Conquer Challenges Perhaps the most inspiring part of Dav's story is the way he has used his own experiences to help others facing comparable challenges. Apart from being enjoyable reads, Dog Man and Captain Underpants also show that kids with dyslexia or attention-deficit/hyperactivity disorder (ADHD) can overcome challenges. They run upon a well-known author who, like them, once struggled in school. They have heard stories about how he was once too lively to take the classroom and was sent to the corridor. They learn that as a child he battled with reading. Nevertheless, he refused to let such challenges stop him. Rather than letting himself get down, he found his path to success using stories, humor, and artistic expression. That is why his writings so greatly influenced. Children can relate to the characters he creates. They feel as though they are understood. They also understand that their difficulties need not be the defining feature of their identity. In Dav's view, that is the most crucial factor. The aim is not just to sell books or make kids laugh. Showing them this helps to prove to them that they can influence their future. He wishes that kids would realize they can utilize their imagination to turn obstacles into possibilities even against great hardship. specifically, that their imaginative capacity is not to be suppressed but rather to be honored. Should his path teach us anything, it is that even the smallest amount of creativity can radically change everything. Apart from being a writer, Dav Pilkey inspires many kids throughout the globe. His works have helped children find pleasure in their challenges, gain confidence in their creative skills, and experience the delight of reading. Every joke, every sketch, and every story he tells helps kids to remember a simple but important reality: their creativity is their strong tool.

CHAPTER TEN

Create Like Dav!

Imagine yourself at your workstation, a blank piece of paper in front of you. Your pencil is in hand and your imagination is running wild. You might see a superhero with a head so large and wobbly, a dog fighting crime, or a villain so absurd he can't even tie his shoes. What if I told you now that this precise moment, the one in which you are just starting, is exactly how Dav Pilkey began his trip? As a kid, he was frequently punished for excessive drawing. A child who let his imagination run wild despite the instructor's warnings to desist is one example. Simply look at where it took him! He did not just grow up to be a writer during his boyhood; he also grew up to inspire millions of kids to pen their narratives. Today is your moment to speak. Guidelines for Creating Your Own Superhero One of the most exciting features of Dav Pilkey's stories is their vibrant and erratic characters. His heroes are not just strong but also funny. From Dog Man to Captain Underpants, his heroes span many genres. There are shortcomings. This is wrong. They don't follow the regulations all the time. Furthermore, this is what distinguishes them so excellent. The question now is, how can one create their superhero? Let's say it out clearly to simplify matters: Start with something funny or surprising first. Consider the qualities distinguishing your hero from others. Imagine them all dressed as a huge banana. They might have superhuman farts. A loud noise can cause them to turn into a pickle. It's better if it's as absurd as possible! Let them have a special talent. What sets your hero apart from others? Can they run quite quickly? Can they shoot spaghetti from their fingertips? Do they wear a mystical cloak letting them fly? Using the ability should be fun, but it should also pose problems as obstacles are what give stories their interest. Build a character fault. Every superhero needs a weakness. Superman's found kryptonite. Spider-Man finds it challenging to take the blame. What about your preferred hero? Most likely, they are afraid of kittens. Maybe they can only use their skills on Tuesdays. They might not be particularly adept at math. Name them something funny or interesting. Among the heroes Dav Pilkey has developed are ones with amusing titles like Captain Underpants, Dog Man, and Super Diaper Baby. Could you come up with a catchy name for your hero? Think about what distinguishes them from others and highlight it! Fifth, pull them! All you have to do is enjoy yourself; don't stress about being a perfect artist! Though lacking in artistry, Dav Pilkey's early sketches were brimming with character. Start with

67

simple shapes, big eyes, and wildly expressive emotions. Drawing should be more enjoyable; your superhero will be more energized to carry out his or her responsibilities. Writing Stories That Will Make People Smile Once you have your superhero, it is time to weave them into a story! Dav Pilkey's books are bursting with all kinds of story twists, humor, and thrilling action. The following is a road map to help you create a narrative that will have readers flipping the pages: Start with a major difficulty. What would you say is the worst thing that might happen to your heroic character? Maybe a hostile creature resembling broccoli is taking control of the school cafeteria. Every time they try to save the day, their underwear may still be getting smaller. A great story usually starts with hardship!

2) Aggravate the circumstances even further. Ensure your hero struggles with the difficulty; else, he may find a simple answer. Deliberately place impediments in their way! They might stumble onto a banana peel. Maybe unintentionally, their sidekick gets them trapped under a massive tortilla. Should the duty be more absurd than it now is, the narrative will be funnier.

3. Add funny conversation. Dav Pilkey's characters always have a funny tone. Composing dialogue would help you to amuse others. Your foe might not

be able to stop sneezing. Could your hero perhaps employ rhymes? Try out different voices and see what makes you chuckle. Utilize the sound effects! Among the most fun things in comics and graphic novels are the sound effects. Boom! "KAPOW!" "SPLORP!" "ALL OUT!" Dav Pilkey's novels are full of words that appear to jump off the page and into the imagination of the reader. Creating your sound effects is one way to bring your narrative to life. Surprise your readers! An excellent book always has unanticipated turns and twists. The antagonist may turn out to be your hero's long-lost pet hamster. Maybe the hero saves by accident.

Try to include a turn that will cause your audience to laugh out loud. Dav Pilkey's Early Years Advice to Artists and Writers Dav Pilkey, the writer, loves to motivate kids to create their narratives. When he talks to young readers, he always makes sure to share these essential bits of advice: Enjoy your mistakes. Some of Dav's most amazing ideas came from mistakes. Who cares if your drawing doesn't look just as you wish it to? Keep going along! Practicing will help you to get better with time. • Act in a genuine way. You should not worry about what others think. If you believe your idea is funny, let your creativity run free. Your mind creates the most interesting stories. • Even when it is difficult, keep creating. Many others warned Dav Pilkey he would fail in his attempts. He did not, nonetheless, cease. If you love painting and writing, don't give up; make sure to keep going! Now is your moment! Now is the moment to create! Start drawing by picking up a pencil, grabbing a sheet of paper, and going to work. Your hero is only waiting to be born into existence. All that remains is to share your story. And you never know. One day, your book might be the one inspiring kids all around the world.

CONCLUSION

Imagine a whole room packed with kids all deeply absorbed in a book. Some people's laughter is so great that they can barely flip the page. Some people are grumbling to themselves, "Just one more chapter!" Then there are those kids who formerly thought they hated reading but are now excitedly flipping the pages of the book with wide-eyed delight. Dav Pilkey's enchantment is shown in this fashion. His books, which have done more than only amuse, have changed fundamentally how children view reading. He has shown children that books are not dull, that tales can be funny and exciting, and that creativity knows no limits. Through humor, adventure, and love, he has shown these qualities.

The road that brought him to be among the most popular writers of children's books, nonetheless, was not simple. Dav Pilkey's story shows the capacity to turn obstacles into strengths, creativity, and perseverance as well as the force of will. The major lesson his life teaches is that being different is not a weakness but rather a superpower. From a small boy in Ohio who couldn't sit still in class to a literary legend worldwide, he traveled. A strong approach is to never give up. As a kid, Dav struggled at school. He was often kicked out of class as his attention-deficit/hyperactivity disorder (ADHD) and dyslexia made it difficult for him to focus. Some of his teachers misread him. Many of his peers mocked him. But Dav found a way to turn those challenges into something extraordinary instead of letting them stop him from reaching his objectives. Sitting in the hallway apart from the other students, he did not feel sorry for himself. Instead, he picked up a pencil and started sketching. He imagined people and saw stories even as he let his imagination go wild. He was doing this without even realizing it, preparing himself for a future in which his wild imagination would become his most valuable quality.

This lesson offers something for everyone—children, parents, instructors, and others. There will always be challenges to conquer not just at the office but also in one's personal life. But instead of seeing them as hurdles we have to conquer, we might decide to see them as opportunities to grow, invent, and find fresh paths to go ahead. The Effect One Character Had on All One of the most amazing things about Dav Pilkey's work is how much one concept—a superhero wearing underwear—can alter everything. Captain Underpants was not just a funny character; he also reflected children's creativity. He was a reflection of the sort of humor kids enjoy but that adults sometimes overlook. Captain Underpants first met resistance. Some grownups thought the books were too stupid and rebellious. The schools even tried to ban them. Young people, though, loved them. Having been misjudged yet never ceased making, two kids identified themselves as George and Harold. Moreover, Dav Pilkey's strong belief in his idea and refusal to let his critics stop him from following it helped Captain Underpants to succeed. It became a global sensation proving that the tales kids love the most are usually those that somewhat depart from the usual flow of events. The growth of graphic novels is changing reading. Dav Pilkey not only authored books but also helped to reimagine what they may be. There was a period when graphic novels were not treated seriously. One set of people thought they were not "real books." Dav, on the other hand, was better informed. Using his work, especially Dog Man, he was able to show the world that graphic novels are a powerful tool for encouraging reading. This allows children who struggle with long text passages to read more effortlessly. Art and narrative together help them to promote creative thinking. They also show that important books need not be traditional. Authors like Dav Pilkey have directly contributed to a notable rise in the number of graphic novels in children's literature. Schools and libraries are adopting them; teachers are using them as teaching resources; kids who once avoided books are now eager to read. That is a sort of legacy that will last for many years to come. How does laughter help people learn? Dav Pilkey's success has been influenced by his capacity to grasp comedy. He knows that kids like to laugh and that their learning is easier as a result. Several studies show that humor can improve memory, increase interest, and make difficult subjects much more accessible. Dav's talent to fill his novels with funny jokes, puns, and surprising situations has turned reading from a boring chore into a thrilling event. Though there are a lot of them, his stories are not all about fart jokes and practical jokes.

They were concerned joy. The aim is to motivate kids to develop a reading habit. Moreover, in a society where many kids struggle with reading, it is a big blessing. Message to Kids: Keep Creating! Should Dav Pilkey wish for kids to take away one thing from his books, it would be this: You, too, can make. Whether they include painting, writing, or the production of magical stories in one's mind, it is essential to recognize and value creative efforts. Creating art does not need permission. You need not wait for someone to tell you that the ideas you have considered are adequate. All you have to do is get started. Dav Pilkey was not the greatest student. He wasn't the greatest when it came to rule adherence. But he was second to none when it came to faith in his creativity. Furthermore, this helped him to be successful. Should you be a child reading this, grab a notepad and start sketching immediately. Design your superheroes from the ground up. Write a story that will have you laughing out loud. Furthermore, if someone says you can't consider Dav Pilkey, the young man who was punished for painting yet finally went on to influence the world. There is a lesson for both instructors and parents: Children should be permitted to read whatever they like. Dav Pilkey's books have prompted adult conversations. Some people were worried they were too chaotic and too absurd. However, his writings motivated kids to read.

The most crucial is that. Not every kid will instantly grow to love classic literature. Some folks need fast, action-packed, enjoyable novels. Unique stories, graphic books, and funny literature help one cultivate a lifetime passion for reading. As parents and educators, our most crucial duty is to support and foster that love. Motivate kids to read several books and support their efforts. Read anything that excites them. Celebrate them instead of trying to restrict their creative powers. This will enable us to keep learning for the whole of our lives. Dav Pilkey's impact will remain with us always. Few writers have had as much impact as Dav Pilkey. His literary works have exposed millions of kids throughout the world. In this manner, they have turned indifferent readers into passionate ones. They have shown kids the worth of their fantasies. What, then, is the most thrilling component? His tale is not yet over. Dav Pilkey will keep creating, inspiring, and showing from here on out that often the greatest stories come from people who reject the standard. Starting as a boy struggling in school and finishing as a world-renowned novelist, this path is proof that success does not always follow a straight road. There are several twists and turns, and sometimes it strays into the corridor. You can achieve all you want if you are tenacious, inventive, and have a good sense of humor. Still, the next time you sit down to write a wacky story or take up a pencil to sketch, remember the most essential lesson Dav Pilkey gave you: Be yourself. Let your mind run wild. And always enjoy yourselves.

Made in the USA
Middletown, DE
29 April 2025